Knights and Castles

Rachel Firth

Illustrated by Sam Church

Reading consultant: Alison Kelly
Roehampton University

Knights lived hundreds
of years ago.

They were special because
they fought on horses.

They could move around
quickly in a fight.

Knights fought with
swords, and long sticks
called lances.

Sword

Lance

They also used daggers, and
heavy clubs called maces.

Mace

Knights used daggers if
they lost their swords.

Knights wore metal clothes to protect themselves.

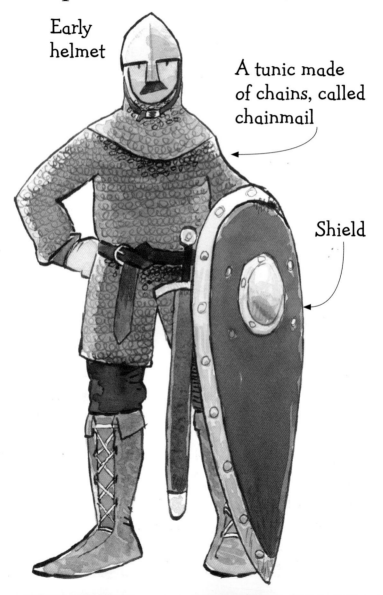

Early helmet

A tunic made of chains, called chainmail

Shield

Later knights wore entire suits made of metal.

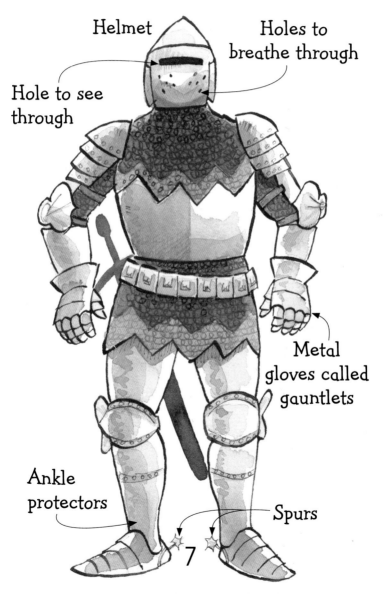

Helmet

Holes to breathe through

Hole to see through

Metal gloves called gauntlets

Ankle protectors

Spurs

7

It took years to be a knight.
At seven years old, you were
a page.

You learned to fight.

You helped to serve food.

After a few years, you
became a squire.

You learned to
use a lance.

You helped to look after the horses.

When a squire was older, he became a knight.

The squire knelt down.

A knight tapped him on his shoulders.

Then he handed the squire a sword and spurs – and the squire was a knight!

10

Sometimes squires were knighted before a battle.

Knights were the most
important fighters in a battle.
Before the battle began,
they lined up.

Then the order was
given... and they charged!

Sharpened
sticks to hurt
the horses

Footsoldiers ran
beside the knights.

People thought knights
should protect women.

They had to be polite, fair and brave at all times.

Some knights were better at this than others.

The most important knight of all was the king. After him came the lords.

Top knight: the king

Important knights: the lords

Most lords owned extra strong homes, called castles.

Less important knights worked for a lord. They lived in his castle.

A lord going into his castle

Ordinary knights

Castles came in all shapes
and sizes. The first castles
were made of wood and earth.

A castle known as a motte
and bailey castle

Bailey
(enclosed area)

Drawbridge

"Motte"
or mound
(hill)

These burned easily, so
lords built castles of stone.

Safe tower, called a keep

Drawbridge

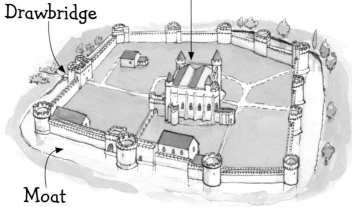

Moat

Over time, lords built
bigger and stronger castles.

A castle had everything that a lord and his family might need.

This castle has had some walls taken away so you can see inside.

The kitchen

Stables

The blacksmith's

Guards keeping watch

21

Sometimes, enemy knights tried to take over a castle.

They used a tower to climb the walls.

They fired huge rocks at the castle.

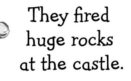

They shot hundreds of arrows.

They hooked
ladders over
the walls.

They attacked the door
with a battering ram.

They dug a tunnel under the
walls to make them fall down.

23

But castles were very
strong and hard to destroy.

Pushing knights off the ladders

Enemy knights
still throwing
stones

There were lots of ways to fight back.

Dropping boiling water on the knights below

Fighting the attackers as they step off the wooden tower

Battering ram breaking through

Knights didn't just fight.
They also loved grand feasts.
They ate all sorts of things
– even peacocks
and swans.

Knights liked to hunt in their spare time. They hunted animals for food and fur.

They also liked to read
and play board games.

Sometimes, knights
held fighting games
called tournaments.

They tried to knock each
other off their horses.

Knights could show off
their fantastic fighting skills.

31

Knights kept their helmets
down in a fight. It was hard
to tell who had won.

So they had patterns or
pictures on their shields to
tell them apart.

These pictures and patterns were called coats of arms.

Every single coat of
arms was different.

Over time, people invented new weapons. Cannons could blast castles to pieces.

Later on, armies began to use handguns.

These were far more dangerous than swords and shields were no help.

Castles and knights were no longer useful. Many castles crumbled and fell into ruins. These days you can visit the ruins...

...and imagine what
it was like to be a knight.

Knight and castle facts

• It could take ten years for 2,000 workers to build a castle.

• Knights' horses cost a lot to buy and feed. Some squires never became knights because they didn't have enough money.

• During tournaments, knights sometimes held mock battles.

• When a knight was away fighting, his wife looked after the castle.

Famous knights

Richard I (1157-1199) was an English king. He fought in wars abroad. He was nicknamed Richard the Lionheart because he was so brave.

Ulrich von Lichtenstein (1200-1278) was an Austrian knight who moved around Europe challenging other knights to fight with him.

El Cid (1043-1099) was a
Spanish knight who rarely
lost a battle.

Jean de Boucicaut
(1366-1421) became a
knight for France when he
was just 16 years old. He
fought against the English
in the Hundred Years' War.

William Marshal (1146-1219), an
English knight, was famous for his
skill at tournaments. He terrified
his enemies on the
battlefield too.

Famous castles

The White Tower is part of the **Tower of London.** It was built by King William I after he invaded England in 1066.

Krak des Chevaliers is a castle in Syria in the Middle East. It was built by a group of knights called the Hospitallers in 1031. At one time, 2,000 knights lived there.

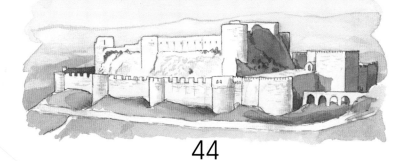

Chillon Castle was built in the early 11th century in Switzerland. It is made up of 100 different buildings.

The Alhambra is a castle in southern Spain.

Its name means 'red palace' because it was built from red bricks.

Malbork Castle is a German castle, built by knights called the Teutonic knights in around 1274.

Castle websites

You can find out more about knights and castles by going to the Usborne Quicklinks Website at **www.usborne-quicklinks.com** and typing in the keywords "first reading knights and castles".

Click on the link for the website you want to visit. Please ask an adult before using the internet.

Index

47

Using the Internet

The recommended websites are regularly reviewed and updated, but please note, Usborne Publishing is not responsible for the content of any website other than its own. We recommend that young children are supervised while using the internet.

Consultant: Dr. Abigail Wheatley

Designed by Louise Flutter
and Sam Chandler
Series designer: Russell Punter
Series editor: Lesley Sims

First published in 2010 by Usborne Publishing Ltd., Usborne House, 83-85 Saffron Hill, London EC1N 8RT, England. www.usborne.com
Copyright © 2010 Usborne Publishing Ltd.